D0773648

Everything You Need to Know About **Peer Pressure**

We all want to be accepted by people we admire.

Everything You Need to Know About *Peer Pressure*

Robyn M. Feller

The Rosen Publishing Group, Inc.
New York

Published in 1993, 1995, 1997, 2001 by The Rosen Publishing Group, Inc.

29 East 21st Street, New York, NY 10010

Library of Congress Cataloging-in-Publication Data

Feller, Robyn M.
Everything you need to know about peer pressure/Robyn M. Feller. — rev. ed.
Includes bibliographical references and index.
ISBN 0-8239-3440-3
Summary: Peer pressure in adolescence—Juvenile literature. 1. Title. II. Series.
HQ777.4.M36 1991 306.85'6—dc20

Manufactured in the United States of America

Contents

Introduction

Amanda had always been a good kid. She got good grades, got along well with her parents and younger sister, and was dedicated to practicing her flute. But Amanda yearned for something different. She was tired of being teased because she was in the band and because she wore girlish clothes that her mom bought for her.

Just a few weeks into her freshman year of high school, Amanda met Jenny. Jenny was very popular and hung out with all of the cool people. Paired up as lab partners, Jenny took a liking to Amanda. She showed Amanda how to apply makeup, what clothes to wear, and encouraged her to quit band. "It's so lame,"

Jenny would say. She also introduced Amanda to new music and books.

Jenny also started taking Amanda along to parties. Amanda thought it was so much fun to dress up in sexy clothes and put on makeup. And she also liked the loads of attention she got from older boys who were at the parties, many of whom attended the local university. And although Amanda knew that her parents would certainly ground her for drinking, smoking, and staying out late, she continued to do it. The most important thing to Amanda was that these people like her and think she was cool, too. And besides, this was her life. She was old enough to make her own decisions. Sometimes she felt bad for lying to her parents, but how could she say no?

Everyone wants to be accepted by people they admire. Some people, especially teens, will do anything to fit in with a group, including drinking, doing drugs, lying to their parents, rejecting childhood friends, and having unsafe sex. This pressure to do things that you might not do on your own is called peer pressure. But this pressure is not always negative. Sometimes peer pressure can have a positive impact on your life. For example, if you join a sports team, it is likely that you will be encouraged by your

Teammates often support and encourage each other to achieve greater levels of success.

peers to be the best you can be. Likewise, joining the debate team may help you become a better student.

Usually, it is fun to be with friends. Friends enjoy activities together and trust each other. But what should you do when some of your friends begin to do things that make you uncomfortable, such as drinking, smoking, or using drugs? What if a friend asks you to help him or her to cheat on a test? Situations like these can make you feel nervous and confused.

Because you are likely to be influenced to some degree by the people you surround yourself with, it is important to choose your friends carefully. Also, when you do find friends that you enjoy, it is important to remember that you should still make your own decisions, especially if you disagree with those that your friends are making. It is important that you feel good about the choices you make. You and your friends don't have to agree or always have the same interests. In fact, a little diversity among friends can add to the enjoyment of the relationship.

This book will discuss the various types of peer pressure that you are likely to face as you get older and how to deal with them. It will also alert you to the ways in which you may be pressuring yourself in order to fit in. And finally, there will be information about making your own choices. This information is intended to help you have the confidence to stand up for your beliefs, interests, and values.

Chapter 1

Peer Pressure in Your Life

People who are similar to you are considered your peers. They may be other students in your school or other people your own age. If you play a sport, athletes who compete at your level are your peers. If you have a job as a stock person in a department store, the other people who work in stock are considered your peers. Unlike your parents or teachers, your peers are people who are in the same situation as you are. They often share similar experiences or lifestyles.

Your friends are probably your closest peers. This group may share common interests and enjoy doing certain things together.

Peer pressure is what causes people to do things that are popular in order to fit in. This pressure can affect

Since your friends are very important to you, you might find yourself wanting to be just like them.

simple things, such as the way you dress, the music you listen to, or even whether or not you take drugs.

Peer pressure is not always bad. If you and your friends think that good grades are important, it may influence you to put more effort into studying. This is positive peer pressure. On the other hand, if your group of friends thinks that stealing is cool and to fit in with them you also begin to steal, this is negative peer pressure. Your peers can have a positive influence when they motivate you to accomplish your goals. But they can also pressure you to do things that you do not want to do. This negative pressure may make you afraid to express an opinion that is different.

What Is Normal?

Growing up involves many changes. Attempting to figure out who you are and what you want to be may cause an enormous amount of stress. You are beginning to take control of your own life and make your own decisions. Sometimes it is difficult to know what choices to make. People often look to their friends to help them make decisions.

A group of friends often shares a similar view of what is acceptable and what is not. Your peer group may seem to be following informal rules. There may be certain things that you have to do in order to fit in. You may feel that you should like certain music or dress in a certain way. Different groups have different preferences. Maybe your friends wear baggy clothes and have tattoos. Or perhaps they listen to country music. To you and your friends, these are just some of the distinctive qualities that make a person part of your group.

If the rules that your group follows fit in with the way you want to live your life, you will be content. However, if the rules of your group do not fit in with the choices you want to make—perhaps you want to do well in school and your friends have started cutting class a lot—it does not mean you are not normal. It means only that you are a little different from those who are closest to you. Also, just because others do

It's okay to be different from your peers.

something does not mean that it is a good thing to do or that it is right. For example, if your friends use illegal drugs, it does not make those drugs any less illegal or any less harmful to your body.

It may be difficult to convince yourself that your friends' behavior is not acceptable. If everyone is drinking, it can't be that big of a deal, right? Or, if all of the people you hang out with lie to their parents about where they go, then it must be okay if you lie to your parents and treat them poorly, right?

It is important, when you find yourself abiding by rules that you don't agree with, to step back and examine why you are going against your own convictions. It isn't easy to go against what everyone else does, but you should feel comfortable about the choices you make. And your friends should respect those choices. You do not need to be exactly like your friends. Learning to express your needs and values is a valuable skill that you will use throughout your life.

Values

You are probably used to parents and teachers telling you the right and wrong things to do. As you grow older, you try to discover values and opinions that are meaningful for you. Making decisions can be difficult. Often it is helpful to talk to friends who are experiencing similar problems. It is easier to talk about your feelings when you can discuss them with friends who are similar to you. Your friends are people you can relate to and trust.

Because your friends' opinions are so valuable, they usually have a great influence over the decisions you make. Your friends can give you the emotional support you need to make it through tough times. They can make you feel comfortable and accepted.

A sense of belonging and identity can also increase your sense of self-esteem, or what you think of yourself. Your friends trust you and talk to you about their problems. Maybe you have faced similar situations. You gain confidence as you try to help them figure out their problems.

Your peer group can greatly influence your values. For instance, if your friends feel that getting good grades is important, they may reinforce the idea for you. If the members of your group think that studying isn't necessary, you may let your grades slide to fit in with them. Or maybe you have never considered volunteering in the community before, but your new friends think that it is a good thing to do. In this way, your peers are influencing your values.

When you feel comfortable with the values that your friends have, positive peer pressure can be helpful. But it is important to recognize if the pressure from your friends becomes negative. You should pay close attention to situations in which your friends want to do things that do not agree with what you believe is right. When these situations arise, a person should decide which values are important to him or her, regardless of what friends think.

Making Your Own Decisions

Joseph had been friendly with Craig since they were small children. They'd grown up playing sports all through elementary and junior high school. Although Joseph didn't want to stop hanging out with Craig, he was concerned because Craig had started using marijuana. Craig had also begun hanging out with kids in the "stoner" crowd; he was excited about his drug-induced experiences.

Craig encouraged Joseph to experience the high. He said that it would expand Joseph's mind and help him see a different reality. But Joseph was committed to following his dream of becoming a professional soccer player and knew that there was no place for drugs in professional athletics. So, despite Craig's urging, Joseph turned him down. To Joseph's surprise, Craig was very understanding and stopped pressuring his friend to use drugs. In fact, if other people would start to harass Joseph about not using, Craig would step in and explain how Joseph was a great soccer player and was going to go to the Olympics someday.

Chapter 2

Giving In to Peer Pressure

Maintaining your individuality in the face of peer pressure can be difficult, especially as a teenager. Up until now, you have probably relied on your family to help you decide what is right for you. They have guided your choices and passed along their values. Now is the time when you will be establishing independence from your parents. It's time for you to make your own choices. Your peers' opinions and values often become more important than those of your family. This is what makes peer pressure so powerful.

It's tough to stand firm on your beliefs when you are simply trying to figure out what they are. Certainly you want to be an individual, but you also want to fit in with your friends. And you must balance that with

the expectations and rules of your family. Now is a critical time to assess yourself and learn to make choices that enhance your life, not ones that stifle it or lead you down a path of self-destruction. You have a responsibility to yourself to decide what is best, now and for your future. Many of the choices you make today will affect the rest of your life.

To help you make good choices, explore the parts of yourself that you like. Are you a talented painter? Take some art classes. Do you love to run in races? Find out when tryouts are for the track team. Do you like to write? Now would be a great time to discover the school newspaper. Pursuing your interests helps build your

self-esteem and develop self-respect, which are important steps in resisting negative peer pressure. Take
Joseph for example: He has a dream of being a professional athlete. He has made a decision not to do drugs
based on respect for himself as an athlete. He has
established his own values. Craig respects Joseph's
decision and wants to see him succeed.

What's in It for You?

*Jeannie is a bright student who cares about her
school. She wants to help make it a better place.
Jeannie wants to be included in the "studious"
group. The students in that crowd get chosen for the
best positions on the newspaper staff and in the
student government. Jeannie knows that teachers
and other students listen to what the studious kids
have to say. The whole school seems to value their
ideas. Jeannie admires what the group has done.*

*More than anything, David wants to be one of the
popular people at his school. He hates being alone.
There is a crowd of guys in his class who are
always hanging out in the lunchroom. They meet in
the afternoon to listen to music and play video
games. They always seem to be having fun together.
They get invited to the coolest parties, and the most
popular girls in school are always around them.*

David wants to be friendly with these popular guys because he's lonely. He wants to fit in and have fun. He wants to belong.

David is more likely to be affected by peer pressure than Jeannie because he doesn't have much respect for his own beliefs and interests. He has yet to develop a solid sense of self that will help him create healthy friendships. He is relying on others to make him feel good about himself. He believes that by being friendly with people he admires, he will be a more interesting and fulfilled person.

Jeannie, on the other hand, has a strong sense of who she is and how she wants to spend her time. She chooses groups that will help her grow and complement her interests.

Jeannie does not need a group for the same reasons David does. She is not looking for direction or emotional support. She is interested in becoming a leader at her school, and she wants to become part of a group because it will help her to reach this goal. She wants friends who share her interests. Her self-confidence helps her to choose friends who will respect her goals.

Self-Esteem and the Family

Your family situation often has a great influence on your self-esteem. In healthy families, parents provide

Your family relationships influence
your self-esteem and confidence.

love, security, and encouragement. They help their
children to grow up with confidence and self-worth.

When you have confidence in yourself, you trust
your instincts. You are more willing to try new things
and less afraid of making mistakes. You are also less
likely to depend on a peer group to make decisions
for you.

When families are not supportive, children get a
different message. If little attention is paid to you at
home, you may think that you don't matter or that
you have failed in some way. You may be more likely
to look to your peers for support. If you join a partic-
ular group because you doubt your own worth, you

may become more dependent on the group. That means you will be more likely to follow that group, regardless of what you think is right for you. It may be more difficult to resist peer pressure.

Types of Negative Peer Pressure

The term "peer pressure" refers to any type of influence that your friends may have over you. Many times, teens are influenced by their peers to do things that result in negative consequences. This is negative peer pressure. Specifically, negative peer pressure refers to activities such as using drugs, alcohol, or cigarettes; vandalizing property; using violence against others; having sex before you are ready or having unsafe sex; stealing; or driving drunk.

Certainly, the opinions of your friends are important, and you want to fit in with them. But if they are influencing you to do things that are destructive, illegal, or unhealthy, it is time to reevaluate why you have chosen to surround yourself with these people. These types of activities can have a negative impact on the rest of your life and you should take them very seriously. You could end up physically injured, in jail, responsible for the injuries of someone else, addicted to drugs, or worse. Is that really the life that you want to lead?

If your friends encourage you to engage in destructive behavior, you could get into trouble.

Remember, the choice is always yours. Even if your friends make bad decisions, it does not mean that you have to go along with them. And if these people will not accept you if you don't participate in activities that you know you shouldn't, it's time to reevaluate those friendships. True friends want the best for you and respect your decisions.

Too Much of a Good Thing

Most people assume that pressure to do well or strive for meaningful goals is always good. For example, if you want to do well in school, you will feel pressure to get good grades. But even positive peer pressure can go too far. If, for instance, you feel worthless unless you always earn As, you may suffer from putting too much pressure on yourself. Or, what if you want to become the best runner on the cross-country team so badly that you work out with an injury and end up being sidelined the entire season? This sort of pressure, although it is to pursue a positive goal, can turn negative if expectations are unrealistic or if they cause you to do things that are unreasonable, such as injuring yourself.

It's important to keep your expectations in perspective. Make sure that you are striving for realistic goals, and be sure to recognize your successes with as much intensity as you recognize your failures.

Fitting In, Standing Out

Within any group, each person generally has his or her position or status. Often, one person will stand out as the leader. He or she has the greatest influence on the rest of the group. Your status within your peer group will affect how much influence your peers have on you as well as how much influence you have on them. If your only priority is to be like the leader because you admire that person, you are going to be greatly affected by the choices that person makes. If, however, you strive toward being yourself, making choices based on your own sense of values, you will have greater self-confidence and will not be as affected by other people's decisions.

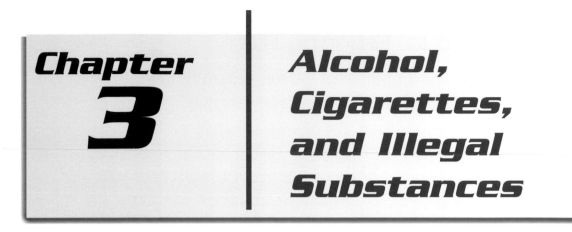

Chapter 3

Alcohol, Cigarettes, and Illegal Substances

Often, a teenager's peers are the first group to introduce him or her to drugs, alcohol, and cigarettes. If a friend starts doing drugs and tells you it's okay to do them, you are more likely to try them. In some peer groups, using drugs is an unwritten rule. Friends may tell you that you are not cool if you don't do drugs, or that you are a coward. Or, they may not say anything—they may just do drugs all the time. Either way, they may be influencing you to use.

Debra had been in high school for six weeks. It was quite a change from junior high. Debra was having a hard time making friends, so when Willow, a girl in her biology class, invited Debra to a party she was giving, Debra was ecstatic. Willow was a junior and very popular. Debra felt honored that Willow had even spoken to her.

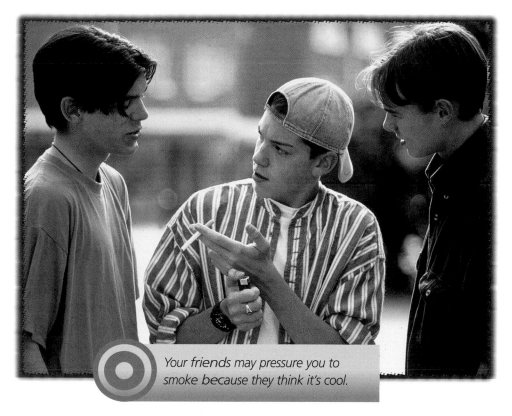

Your friends may pressure you to smoke because they think it's cool.

When Debra arrived at the party, she felt out of place. A lot of people were drinking, and Debra had never been interested in alcohol. She spotted some other freshmen she knew in a corner and went over to talk to them.

Then Willow came up and pulled Debra away from the group. "Hey, what are you doing hanging out with those losers, Deb?" she asked. "You're too cool for that." Debra thought of disagreeing but decided against it. Being seen with Willow made her feel cool.

Willow led Debra into another room. "This is where the action is," she said. Debra saw a bunch of people sitting in a circle. Then she noticed the smell of pot and saw people passing around a joint.

"Have a seat, Deb," Willow said. She sat down and made room in the circle for Debra.

Debra had never smoked pot before. She didn't really want to try it, but she didn't want to seem judgmental either. She felt nervous, but sat down anyway.

After smoking for a while, Debra felt strange and uncomfortable. She sat a little outside the circle, staring at the people talking, but she could not understand what was going on. She was so depressed and unhappy that she left the party early.

The next day, Debra decided that pot was not her thing. She didn't understand how people could be stoned and still socialize. While she was sober, she felt out of place. But once she'd smoked, she felt awful. Debra didn't care if Willow thought that she wasn't cool. She decided that she would rather be uncool than unhappy.

Debra was influenced by peer pressure to try marijuana. She didn't want to try it, but she thought it would make people believe that she was cool.

Debra learned a powerful lesson: Being pressured into doing something you don't want to do will likely end up causing you problems. This is certainly true where drugs are concerned. Drugs can cause you to do things you wouldn't normally do, things that you will later regret. Drugs are often addictive, bad for your health, and illegal. If you feel pressured into taking drugs, think about the person who is pressuring you. Is he or she really your friend? Does he or she just want someone to do drugs with? The old saying "misery loves company" is true where drugs are concerned. If a drug user can get other people to use with him or her, it may help that person feel better about himself or herself. Or maybe the person wants to sell drugs to you. If the person can get you to use regularly, he or she will profit.

People who pressure you to use drugs are not doing so out of concern for you. They are motivated instead by self-interest, insecurity, or financial gain. A question to consider: Would this person want to hang out with you if you were not using drugs? Or, would you want to hang out with him or her? If not, realize that this person is not your friend. If so, think about waiting until the person is sober and find ways to have fun together without drugs.

If you think that a friend has a drug problem, you should encourage him or her to seek help. Joining him or her by using drugs will only cause problems for both of you. You will be a better friend by helping your friend to recover.

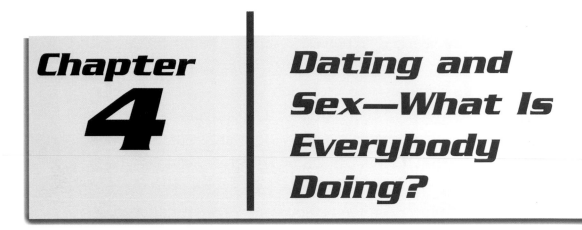

Chapter 4

Dating and Sex—What Is Everybody Doing?

Many teenagers think that dating and having sex will make them seem mature. But dating and sex require responsibility first.

Romantic and sexual feelings are a natural part of growing up. When you are ready to begin a sexual relationship, there are serious things that you need to think about. These include birth control, pregnancy, sexually transmitted diseases (STDs), including AIDS, personal values, and commitment.

Peer groups often talk about dating. You may feel more comfortable talking about it with people your own age. But sometimes there can be pressure. They may tell you when and with whom you should be having a relationship. But everyone is different. People develop at different rates, emotionally and physically. What is right for one person may not be right for everyone. It's important that you decide to do what makes you feel comfortable and safe.

Dating is a natural part of growing up.

Pressure from Friends

Your friends may talk with each other about dating or sex. It is often easier to talk about these things with people your own age. Your friends may tell you of their experiences or offer you advice.

Often, hearing your friends talk about dating or sex can make you feel pressured. If you are the only one of your friends who is not dating, you may feel left out. Or maybe you feel that you are the only one of your friends who has not had sex.

Being different from the group can make anyone feel pressured to fit in. But you must be the one to make the actual decision. It is okay to postpone dating or sex. Whatever you choose, it is important for that decision to be your own.

Jennifer met Alan at a school dance. Even though they were in the same class, they had never spoken. Now, Alan was constantly calling her and taking her places. Jennifer had never had a boyfriend before, and she really liked being with Alan. All of her friends had boyfriends, and the couples often went out together. When Jennifer wasn't with Alan, she was on the phone with her friends. They would talk about their boyfriends and make plans.

After they had been dating for several months, Alan and Jennifer started fighting most of the time. He didn't like hanging out with her friends. He wanted to play basketball with his buddies, something he hadn't done in weeks. Jennifer thought he was being selfish. What was she supposed to tell her friends when she showed up alone?

Finally, Alan broke up with Jennifer. She was devastated. She liked having someone who made her feel special. Jennifer hated the idea of being alone. The thought made her depressed. So, when her friend Dana mentioned that Billy seemed friendly, she set to work immediately to make him her boyfriend.

Jennifer thought she needed a boyfriend to be happy and feel good about herself. If someone else thought she was special, it must be true. What Jennifer might not realize is that it is healthy to spend time alone. It can be a time to remember all those reasons why you are special on your own. Also, if you feel uncomfortable when you are alone, you may want to examine why. Perhaps there are some things that are bothering you that you have not wanted to face. Time alone can give you a chance to deal with problems in your life.

Right for You

Simon was seventeen and tired of being teased because he was a virgin. All of his friends were

Even if all of your friends are dating, you should postpone romance until it feels comfortable.

involved in sexual relationships. But Simon insisted that he was waiting to meet a girl he loved and felt comfortable with. He didn't feel ready yet.

One weekend, he went on a camping trip with his family and saw Donna. He knew Donna from school. She asked Simon to come with her and look at the stars. Once they were away from every-body, Donna began to touch him and tell him how good-looking he was. Simon was surprised. It made him uncomfortable, but he did not tell her to stop because he did not want Donna to know that he was a virgin. He was tired of people thinking that he was innocent. He decided to go along and began touching Donna. Even though he knew it was not what he wanted, he and Donna had sex.

The next day, he thought about Donna on the drive home. He was upset with himself for having had sex for the first time with somebody he was not in love with. He had done it only because he didn't want to be teased anymore for being a virgin.

Simon reacted to Donna the way he thought his friends would. But, by going against what he thought was right, Simon did something he didn't want to do and wasn't prepared for. He was trying to fit in with his friends rather than trusting what he really felt.

There is nothing wrong with waiting for a time that feels more appropriate for you. Not everyone is ready to have a serious relationship during the teenage years. But that doesn't mean you will never be ready. Decide what you feel is right for yourself. Relying too heavily on your peer group can make you ignore your own judgment. The decision to be sexually active is a choice that only you can make.

Your Peer Group and Sex

As a teen, your body undergoes a maturing process, with many physical and emotional changes. You are beginning to see yourself as a sexual person who is able to enjoy sexual behavior. Sexual behavior, however, includes much more than sexual intercourse. It can mean holding hands, kissing, cuddling, or touching. As you begin to explore your own sexuality, your peer group may have a strong influence on you. You will have to make important decisions about dating and sex. Before you listen to your friends' advice, look closely at what sexuality means to your peer group. Does your peer group use sex to:

◎ **Be popular?**

◎ **Get even with someone else?**

◎ **Escape from problems?**

◎ **Improve self-esteem?**

◎ **Appear more grown up?**

Think about your own expectations about dating and sex. Ask yourself what you want and what you don't want. You may not agree with what your peer group is suggesting, and that's okay. Sex is a serious and personal matter. You need to know about birth control and how to protect yourself from sexually transmitted diseases (STDs). If you do decide to become sexually active, you can lower the risk of pregnancy and contracting STDs by using condoms. But only abstaining from sex—not having sex—offers

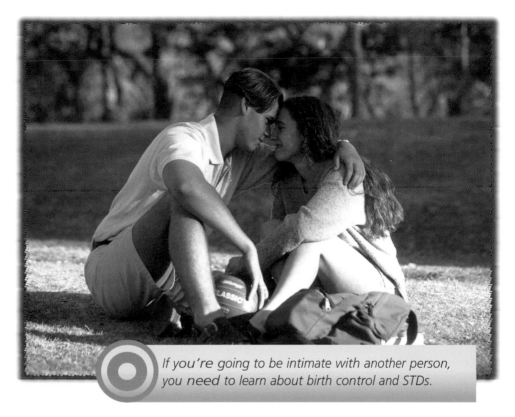

If you're going to be intimate with another person, you need to learn about birth control and STDs.

complete protection. It can be difficult to be abstinent when your friends are not, but more and more teens are making this choice because of the risks posed by sex. You are the one who must live with the consequences of your choices, not your peer group. Make your decisions with that in mind.

Date Rape

Susan had always admired Michael. He was a senior and the star of the football team. Susan tried to be wherever she thought Michael might be. One night after a game, she waited for him to

come out of the locker room. When he finally did, she built up enough courage to talk to him. He asked her to go for a drive with him, and Susan agreed right away. They talked about the game as they drove out into the woods.

Michael wasn't really interested in talking about the game. He was thinking about his friends. They were all so impressed by him. They all thought that he could have sex with any girl he wanted. They didn't know how many times Michael had been turned down. And Michael didn't want them to know. He had a reputation to protect.

After he parked his truck, Michael asked Susan to go for a walk. When they reached a clearing, he started to kiss her. Susan kissed him back. But then he started grabbing her breasts and trying to unzip her jeans. Susan begged him to stop. But Michael just pushed her to the ground and forced Susan to have sex with him. On the ride home, she was so afraid that she couldn't speak. Michael told her not to tell anyone as he kissed her good night.

When Michael told his friends about Susan, he really played it up. He lied and told them that she was all over him and she wanted him to have sex with her. His friends were impressed.

Michael knew that Susan admired him and used that to his advantage. But having sex with someone against his or her will is rape. When this happens between people who know each other, like Michael and Susan, it is called date rape. Susan got into Michael's truck willingly. But she did not want to have sex.

Rape is a violent crime. Having sex with anyone who says no is rape. Even if a person is dressed in sexy clothing or has agreed to other kinds of touching, he or she still has the right to refuse sex. It doesn't matter that Susan agreed to get into the car alone with Michael. It also doesn't matter if someone is drunk or high on drugs. When someone says no, it means no. There is no excuse for not listening.

Why did Michael rape Susan? He may have thought she really wanted to have sex because she liked him and was always hanging around him. She also agreed to get into his truck and let him kiss her. But he was not listening when she told him to stop. Michael was more interested in his reputation than in Susan. Everybody thought he was so cool and popular. He felt like he needed to live up to their expectations. His friends expected him to have sex with many girls.

When people act a certain way to fit in with a crowd's expectations, they can hurt themselves or others. Even though teens may feel pressured by their peers, they are still responsible for their own actions.

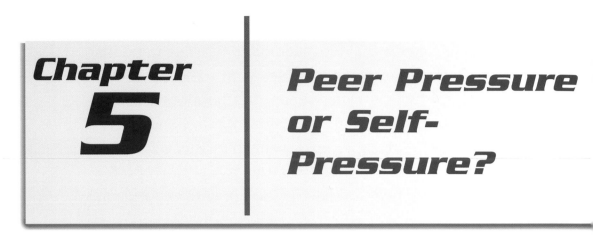

Chapter 5

Peer Pressure or Self-Pressure?

Almost everyone can give an example of a phrase that implies peer pressure. "Everybody's doing it." "What are you—chicken?" "Aren't you cool?" All these statements are obviously pressuring.

But you do not have to be directly challenged to do something in order to feel pressured. Even if nobody tells you to do things that the group does, you can feel pressured anyway. Teens feel pressured to fit in with their friends when they are afraid of being left out. Being different from the group can make some teens feel awkward.

It can be very difficult to recognize and say no to unspoken peer pressure. If someone tells you to do something, you can always say no. But how do you say

no when you haven't been asked? What do you do
when your group sets unspoken rules that you do not
want to follow?

*Marcia didn't like cigarettes. Her father's
smoking had caused him to develop lung cancer.
Marcia didn't like the smell, the smoke, or the
tobacco stains. She knew that cigarettes could
ruin people's health. Although she was used to
being around smoke at home, she never wanted
to try smoking.*

*Marcia was an artist, and she hung out with
the other artists at her school. Her friends were
very supportive and intelligent. They worked
hard at their interests and never pressured her
into things she didn't want to do. She always felt
comfortable around them.*

*However, Marcia began to notice a trend in her
group of friends. One by one, they were beginning to smoke. Soon Marcia found that she was
the only person in her circle of friends who didn't
puff away, at least occasionally. Eventually, most
of her friends were smoking all the time.*

*Marcia found herself constantly surrounded
by cigarette smoke. Her father still smoked
despite his cancer, and now all her friends did
as well.*

Soon, Marcia began to regard smoking in a different light. It did not seem so odd. After all, she had grown up around it. Instead of considering it stupid, she began to think of smoking as something all artists did. She felt out of place when her friends discussed the trials and tribulations of their habit. It made her feel like she wasn't part of the group anymore.

Not surprisingly, Marcia started smoking.

Peers don't always actively tell you to do things. They don't need to. If all your friends smoke, or do drugs, eventually you will begin to associate that habit with your group of friends. A habit you once thought was silly or stupid may start to seem cool.

When each of your friends does something regularly, that action becomes legitimized in your mind. The actions of your friends will start to seem normal.

Unspoken peer pressure is hard to combat. It's not the fault of your friends; after all, they aren't telling you to do anything.

People often want to be like their friends. That's why the members of a peer group often dress similarly. They want to be identified with their friends.

Often, people feel that being in a group gives them a certain identity. People who enjoy the same things, such as sports or art, will want to be in a group whose members have a reputation for being "jocks" or "artists."

Very often, teenagers will dress alike to show a sense of identity, pride, and solidarity with their peers.

Categories like these are stereotypes. Everybody has certain ideas about what a "nerd," "preppie," "stoner," or "hippie" is like.

Trying to fit into a stereotype can be a type of unspoken peer pressure. In order to become a member of a group, or clique, you may feel that you have to do certain things. You may attempt to become the stereotype.

This type of pressure can cause a lot of stress. Nobody is, or should strive to be, a stereotype. There are things that make everybody in a group different. Often, these stereotypes involve expectations that do not fit with who you really are. When this happens, you may feel pressured to do something that you do not truly want to do.

It is very hard to ignore unspoken peer pressure. But you should remember that your personality is unique and valuable. It can be fun to be with friends who have things in common with you. But you should not feel that everybody has to be the same. Becoming a stereotype can hide some of the things that make you who you are.

Chapter 6

Making Your Own Decisions

Often, you may not want to do what your friends are doing. Maybe they're smoking, and you hate the very smell of cigarette smoke. Maybe your group loves pop music, and you prefer jazz. Or perhaps your group makes a habit of cutting classes, but grades are important to you. Some of your friends may do drugs, while you think using drugs is dangerous.

Saying No Is Not Easy

Whatever your group may be doing, saying no may be difficult. You know that if you go along, your group is more likely to accept you. You also know that when you try to break away from the "rules," you risk being left out.

Peer pressure makes these choices very difficult. But you do not have to go along with anything that makes you feel uncomfortable. You can't be expected to agree with everything that the rest of the group wants. Every person is unique.

Dare to Be Different

It takes a lot of courage to be yourself. But it can also bring you great satisfaction. Following your own beliefs will make you more independent. It will give you control over your own actions.

Allowing yourself to be different helps you to figure out who you are. You may be able to try new things that you might never have done if you only followed the group. Being independent allows you to find the activities, opinions, and tastes that you like the most and that best reflect your personality. It gives you the confidence to control your decisions and goals.

Discovering Yourself

Sharon had begun wondering if her friends were really right for her. They had been together since junior high. They knew everything about each other, but lately Sharon had begun wondering what she was going to do after graduation. She didn't think that she and her friends shared the same goals anymore. She had been thinking about going to college, but she knew that her friends would just laugh if she told them. They wanted to stay in their small town. Sharon was scared; she wanted to make plans for her future but was afraid of losing her friends.

One day there was a meeting at school for a college Sharon was interested in. She met some of the students who attended the college and was surprised to find she felt very comfortable with them. Soon she found herself laughing at their jokes. Sharon was also impressed by the way they talked about their future plans. When they invited her to come with them to the movies that night, she eagerly accepted. Sharon felt happier with herself and more confident about her future.

As you mature, you may find yourself outgrowing past relationships. This is common, but it can be very difficult. Changing your group of friends may mean parting with people you have been close to for many years. It may feel as if you are losing part of your identity.

People are constantly changing and growing. Your interests and priorities will also change. If you find that you are losing interest in the things your friends want to do or if you want to try something new, it may be time for a change. You can make new friends with whom you have more in common. New friends may be what you need as you set new goals and think about the future.

Positive Peer Pressure

Although peer pressure has its negative side, young people can also influence each other in positive ways.

It is normal to develop your own plans and goals, even if they differ from those of your peer group.

Teenagers set examples for their friends when they encourage others to do their best in school, to stay away from smoking, drinking, and drugs, and to participate in fun, healthy activities.

Peer Counseling

In many schools, groups of teens become peer counselors (also called peer partners, peer helpers, natural helpers, or peer facilitators). These young people are trained to listen and respond to other teens.

Sometimes it's hard for teenagers to express their fears, problems, or deepest thoughts. Peer counselors can relate to what other young people are going through. They learn to be sensitive to the emotional needs of others and help their schoolmates to talk about their feelings. They also help them with decisions and show them what options are available.

Peer counselors can talk about many kinds of problems. Teens speak with them about relationships with parents or friends. They talk about pressures to drink or have sex. Peer counselors may hear stories of depression, loneliness, or even abuse.

Peer counselors can offer common-sense advice. Troubled students may look to counselors for suggestions. For other young people, just being able to talk about their concerns improves the quality of their lives.

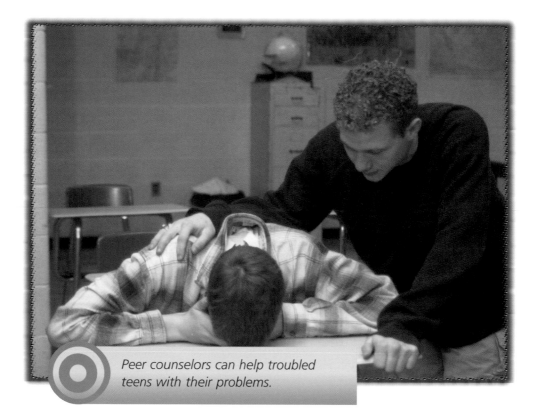

Peer counselors can help troubled teens with their problems.

Resolving Conflicts

Students Against Violence Everywhere (SAVE) and Peace by Peace are two popular programs that are used today in many high schools to help combat school violence. Both programs use peer mediation to stop violence. Teens who participate as mediators are trained to listen to other students and to help them resolve conflicts. Instead of using fists or weapons to solve arguments, students sit down and talk to one another calmly. They try to work things out with the help of a mediator. Many high schools involved in these programs have seen their levels of violence drop dramatically, easing tension and pressure for everyone.

Other groups throughout the country have been successful in working with students. STOPP (Students To Offset Peer Pressure) offers alternatives and advice to teens who are dealing with negative peer pressure. SADD (Students Against Driving Drunk) uses positive peer pressure to inform young people about the dangers of drinking and driving. Just Say No is a program that informs young people about the dangers of drug use. It shows teens alternatives to using drugs and alcohol.

All of these groups help teens to cope with life's pressures while learning problem-solving skills. Teens involved in these groups also learn to be supportive of others. Most of all, they gain maturity and independence. They feel a sense of responsibility to other young people who are looking to them for support and direction at difficult times in their lives.

Chapter 7 | The Choice Is Yours

Everyone has felt pressured by his or her peers at some point. Even adults experience peer pressure. Peer pressure becomes negative when it causes you to do something that is unhealthy or dangerous. People who allow themselves to be pressured by their peers are often afraid of being unpopular or alone. They may feel that keeping their friends, no matter what it takes, will make them feel better about themselves. But following the group in this way allows other people to make your decisions for you. Developing positive self-esteem can help you to resist pressure from friends. Positive self-esteem allows you to feel good about yourself, regardless of what others think.

Feeling Good About Yourself

Work at thinking positively about yourself. Think about all the things that you do well; maybe you can

A part-time job can increase your sense of self-esteem and ability to think independently.

paint, sing, or make people laugh. Your talents, such as drawing, playing basketball, or dancing, can make you feel better about yourself and allow others to appreciate you for who you are.

Set goals for yourself. Don't make them unreachable—set goals you know you can achieve. For instance, a goal could be getting a grade higher than a C on your next history test. Congratulate yourself when you meet the goal.

Remember that other people will be there for you if you need help. Talk about your problems with your parents, friends, teachers, counselors, or religious leaders. Other sources of support are listed in the back of this book.

Do things that make you feel good about yourself, such as trying out for a school play, volunteering to help behind-the-scenes, or starting a hobby like playing the guitar. Helping others and developing your own skills always makes you feel good about yourself. A part-time job can increase your sense of responsibility and independence.

It is better to have positive self-esteem than to depend on the approval of others. You will gain more confidence and control over your life. You will have the power to accept or reject what others think of you. Be proud of who you are and what you can accomplish.

You Can Do It

Being mature and acting responsibly are two of the most difficult things that can be asked of anyone. Learning to trust your own judgment is a stressful, but rewarding, experience. Don't let others pressure you into doing things that are not right for you. Make your own decisions.

Being mature means having the ability to be both a good friend and an independent individual. It can be fun to be a part of a group, but be aware if friendships are no longer comfortable. This may happen if your friends begin to do things that you do not agree with. Remember that you are always in control and have other choices. The most important element is to have a strong sense of your own individuality.

Glossary

adolescence Period of growth between childhood and adulthood.

clique A small, exclusive group of people.

conformity Going along with what others are doing in order to be liked or accepted by them.

crowd A large group of people with things in common.

date rape Forced sex between two people who know each other.

emotional support Listening to, or encouraging someone, with regard to his or her feelings.

instincts Strong motivations or impulses that you have naturally within yourself.

negative Having a bad or unfavorable effect.

peer group A group of friends or classmates who

have things in common.

peer pressure   Force or encouragement by friends to do certain things or to act a certain way.

positive   Having a good or favorable effect.

self-esteem   One's feeling of confidence or personal worth.

sexuality   Interest in sex; sexual drive or activity.

status   One's position or rank in relation to others.

values   The beliefs that a person holds.

Where to Go for Help

Check your local library or phone book for listings of crisis intervention centers and hotlines for counseling or referrals. You may also want to talk to your school guidance counselor. Ask if your school has a peer-counseling program.

In the United States

Al-Anon/Alateen
1600 Corporate Landing Parkway
Virginia Beach, VA 23456
(757) 563-1600
(888) 4ALANON (425-2666)
Web site: http://www.al-anon.org

American Social Health Association
P.O. Box 13827
Research Triangle Park, NC 27709
(919) 361-8400
Web site: http://www.ashastd.org

The Bureau for At-Risk Youth
135 Dupont Street
P.O. Box 760
Plainview, NY 11803-0760
(800) 99-YOUTH (999-6884)
Web site: http://www.at-risk.com

Covenant House
346 West 17th Street
New York, NY 10011
(800) 999-9999
Web site: http://www.covenanthouse.org

Girls' Circle Association
37 Bonnie Brae
Novato, CA 94949
(415) 388-0644
(415) 267-5224
Web site: http://girlscircle.com

Join Together
441 Stuart Street
Boston, MA 02116
(617) 437-1500
Web site: http://www.jointogether.org

In Canada

The Duke of Edinburgh's Award
Young Canadians Challenge
207 Queen's Quay West
Suite 450
P.O. Box 124
Toronto, ON M5J 1A7
(800) 872-DUKE (3853)
(416) 203-2282
Web site: http://dukeofed.org

Justice for Children and Youth
Canadian Foundation for Children, Youth and the Law
720 Spadina Avenue, Suite 405
Toronto, ON M5S 2T9
(416) 920-1633

Ontario Public Health Association
468 Queen Street East, Suite 202
Toronto, ON M5A 1T7
(416) 367-3313
(800) 267-6817
Web site: http://www.opha.on.ca

For Further Reading

Eager, George. *All About Peer Pressure*. Valdosta, GA: Mailbox Club Books, 1994.

Glass, George. *Drugs and Fitting In*. New York: Rosen Publishing Group, 1998.

Havelin, Kate. *Peer Pressure: How Can I Say No?* Mankato, MN: LifeMatters, 2000.

McCoy, Kathy, and Charles Wibbelsman. *Life Happens: A Teenager's Guide to Friends, Failure, Sexuality, Love, Rejection, Addiction, Peer Pressure, Families, Loss, Depression, Change, and Other Challenges of Living*. New York: Berkeley Publishing Group, 1996.

Pogány, Susan Browning. *SexSmart: 501 Reasons to Hold Off on Sex*. Minneapolis, MN: Fairview Press, 1998.

Scott, Sharon. *How to Say No and Keep Your Friends: Peer Pressure Reversal for Teens and Preteens*. 2nd ed. Amherst, MA: Human Resources Development Press, 1997.

Index

About the Author

Robyn M. Feller is a writer, researcher, and editor in New York City. She holds a degree in English literature and rhetoric from the State University of New York at Binghamton. She also studied communications at Hunter College.

Photo Credits

Cover © Peter Langone/International Stock; pp. 2, 48, 50 by Antonio Mari; pp. 8, 53 © Skjold Stock Photography; p. 11 © Van Steyn/Pictor; p. 13, 37 © Bob Daemmrich/The Image Works; pp. 18, 27, 34, 43 © Telegraph Colour Library/FPG; p. 21 © Mike Malyszko/FPG; p. 23 © Mark Reinstein/Pictor; p. 31 © Esbin-Anderson/The Image Works.

Design and Layout

Thomas Forget